S T A R T I N G   P O I N T S

AIR

Su Swallow

Photography by Chris Fairclough

FRANKLIN WATTS
LONDON · NEW YORK · SYDNEY · TORONTO

© 1990 Franklin Watts

First published in Great Britain in 1990 by
Franklin Watts
96 Leonard Street
London EC2A 4RH

First published in Australia by
.Franklin Watts Australia
14 Mars Road
Lane Cove
N.S.W. 2066

First published in the United States by
Franklin Watts Inc.
387 Park Avenue South
New York, NY 10016

UK ISBN: 0 7496 0231 7

A CIP Catalogue record for this book is available from the British Library.

Series design: David Bennett
Model making: Stan Johnson
Picture Research: Sarah Ridley
Typesetting: Lineage, Watford
Printed in Belgium

Additional photographs: Heather Angel 22 (all), 23 (inset); Ardea 7t; Chris
Fairclough Colour Library 4-5, 6t, 7cl, 12t, 12cl, 17 (inset), 21b, 23, 28t, 29t;
Frank Lane Picture Library 6b, 7cr, 8t, 8br, 9 (inset), 12b, 13tl, 29b; Hutchison
Library 21tr, 28br; Natural History Photographic Agency 9; Rex Features 21tl;
South American Pictures 20bl; ZEFA 7b, 8bl, 13tr, 13bl, 13br, 15, 16 (all), 17, 20t,
20br, 28bl.

Acknowledgements: ''Walking in the Air'' by Howard Blake from the Snowman.
© 1982 by Highbridge Music. Reproduced by permission of
Faber Music Ltd. ''A Hot Day'' by A. S. J. Tessimond from
''The Collected Poems of A. S. J. Tessimond''. © Hubert Nicholson.

CONTENTS

Summer Air

A Hot Day

Cotton wool clouds loiter.
A lawnmower, very far,
Birrs. Then a bee comes
To a crimson rose and softly
Deftly and fatly crams
A velvet body in.

A tree, June-lazy, makes
A tent of dim green light.
Sunlight weaves in the leaves,
Honey-light laced with leaf-light,
Green interleaved with gold.
Sunlight gathers its rays
In sheaves, which the wind unweaves
And then reweaves – the wind
That puffs a smell of grass
Through the heat-heavy, trembling
Summer pool of air.

A.S.J. Tessimond

Air For Life

People, plants and animals must breathe air to live.

The Earth is surrounded by a layer of air, which is a mixture of gases. When we breathe, our bodies take in oxygen and give out another gas called carbon dioxide. Air is usually invisible, but you can see your warm breath on a cold day.

Animals, like people, take in oxygen from the air and breathe out carbon dioxide. Plants use the air to make their food, but they take in carbon dioxide and give out oxygen. So plants help to keep the right balance of gases in the air. Without trees, shrubs and other plants there would not be enough oxygen for us to breathe.

Plants are important for the air in another way, too. When large areas of trees are cut down, for example when rainforests are cleared for farming, carbon dioxide builds up in the air. This gas absorbs heat from the Sun and stops it escaping back into Space. The Earth's atmosphere is slowly warming up.

Animals that live in water breathe in different ways. Whales come to the surface to breathe, and blow out air through a blowhole on the top of their head. Fish breathe by taking in air which is dissolved in the water. Water goes in through the mouth and out through the gills, which remove oxygen. The water spider lives in a bubble of air which it collects from the surface.

People cannot breathe under water, so divers carry air in bottles.

In Flight

Some animals can fly through the air. Others can glide.

Birds have light, streamlined bodies which fly easily through the air. As their wings go up, the feathers twist open to let the air pass through. As the wings go down, the feathers overlap to push against the air.

Swifts spend more time in the air than other birds. They spend most of the year on the wing, catching insects and even resting in the air.

Hummingbirds hover by flapping their wings backwards and forwards very fast. Their wings make a humming noise as they beat up to 100 times a second. These tiny birds feed on nectar from flowers.

Insects, like birds, have wings. Every year, millions of monarch butterflies fly from North America to spend the winter in Mexico, 3000 km away.

A few animals, like this flying squirrel, have flaps of skin on either side of their bodies to help them glide through the air.

Bats are the only mammals that can really fly. They have broad wings of thin skin. The long-eared bat (below) flies in the late evening. In winter it hibernates in caves and cellars.

Paper Planes

Try making shapes out of paper that will fly and float through the air. Test different kinds of paper to see which work best. See if you can design your own paper plane.

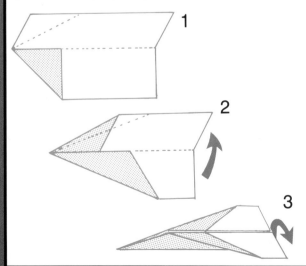

To make a paper glider, fold an A4 sheet of paper in half lengthways. Open it out and fold the two front corners in to the centre fold (1). Now fold the new corners in to the centre and fold the paper in half again along the centre fold (2). Fold down the wings (3).

Point the glider upwards slightly and launch it smoothly into the air.

To make a paper parachute, cut a square of tissue paper. Tape a thread to each corner and tie a weight to the ends. Drop the parachute from a height. Then cut a hole in the top of the parachute and see how it falls. Try making round parachutes, too, and test different weights.

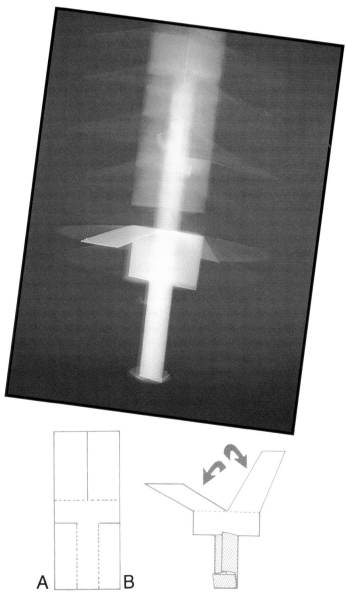

To make a paper helicopter, you need a piece of paper about 15 cm by 5 cm. Then follow these steps:

1 Make three cuts.
2 Fold flaps A and B in so that they overlap. Fold up the bottom of this strip.
3 Fold the two strips at the top down, one forward and one back.

Drop the helicopter from a height and watch it spin as it falls.

A   B

Wind And Weather

Moving air, called wind, can shape the land in many ways. It can also cause serious damage.

Fierce winds bring huge waves crashing on to the shore. The water washes over the land and wears away the coastline.

On a hot day, a gentle breeze helps to keep us cool. A stronger wind blows the washing dry. In a storm, gale force winds can uproot trees, wreck ships and destroy homes.

The strength of winds is measured on the Beaufort Scale, invented by a British admiral. The scale runs from 0, a calm day, to 12, a hurricane. Hurricanes, also called cyclones and typhoons, can blow at up to 300 km an hour.

Trees that grow near the coast may be misshapen. They are bent over by the force of the wind blowing inland from the sea.

When it snows, the wind may pile the snow up into deep snowdrifts, which block roads and railways.

Sand is always on the move, blown about by the wind. Sand dunes are often planted with marram grass to hold them in place.

A tornado is a whirlwind which looks like a funnel of cloud. It can cause terrible damage as it races across the land. The biggest trees, the heaviest lorries, the strongest buildings may all be swept aside in a fierce wind storm. People and animals may be killed as they are hit or crushed by flying debris.

Making Kites

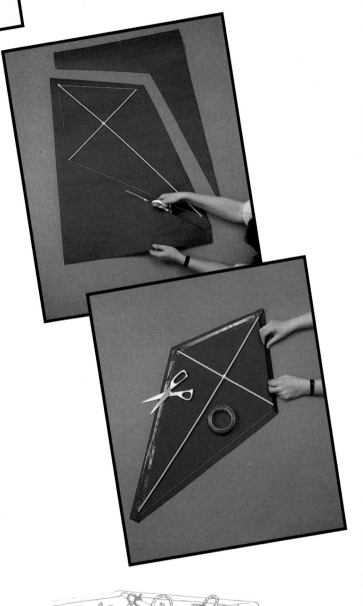

90 cm

45 cm

To make a simple kite, start by making the frame. Cut two pieces of thin dowel, one 90 cm long and the other 45 cm long. Tie or tape them together so they cross one third of the way down the long dowel. Now run a long piece of string from one dowel end to the next, binding or glueing it firmly each time, to make a diamond-shaped frame.

Lay the frame on a large sheet of strong paper and cut round the frame, allowing an extra 3 cm all round.

Fold the edges over the string frame and glue or tape them down firmly and neatly.

Make four small holes 15 cm from the centre of the cross. Cut four pieces of string 30 cm long and fix one to the dowel by each hole (picture 1). Thread the four strings through to the other side.

Join the four pieces of string to a curtain ring, and attach a reel of string to the ring, too (2).

1

2

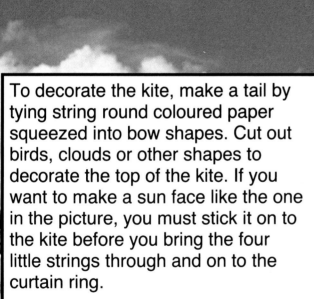

To decorate the kite, make a tail by tying string round coloured paper squeezed into bow shapes. Cut out birds, clouds or other shapes to decorate the top of the kite. If you want to make a sun face like the one in the picture, you must stick it on to the kite before you bring the four little strings through and on to the curtain ring.

Try your kite out on a windy day, in an open space. To launch it, ask a friend to throw the kite in the air while you hold the reel a few metres away. Let out more string as the wind catches the kite and pulls it up.

Floating On Air

People cannot fly like birds but they can use wind and air currents to carry them through the sky.

A glider has no engine. It is pulled up into the air by a plane. Then it uses air currents to keep it airborne.

A hang-glider leaps into the air from a hill or cliff. Wind fills the glider wing and keeps it aloft.

When a parachute opens it fills with air, which slows the person's fall.

Hot air rises. When a hot air balloon is filled with air heated by a gas burner (right, inset) it rises from the ground. It flies until the air inside cools down.

Mobiles

Mobiles twist and turn when the air round them moves. Try decorating a room with one.

Wind chime

Cut about six pieces of invisible thread or pretty ribbon, each about 60 cm long. Thread small colourful or shiny objects – buttons, bells, bottle tops and other odds and ends – on to the thread or ribbon, tying each in place with a knot. Tie or tape the top end of each thread round a piece of balsa wood or along a coat hanger so that the objects just touch. Hang your wind chime near a window so it moves gently.

Sky mobile

What might you see in the sky? Write down a few ideas and design your own mobile. Cut the shapes out of stiff paper or thin card, which is folded so you make two of each shape. Fix one of each shape on to pieces of cotton or invisible thread, using clear tape. Glue the matching shapes in place.

Air For Sound

All kinds of musical instruments use air to make their sounds.

Wind instruments such as pipes and flutes are among the oldest known musical instruments. Today, people all round the world still make music by blowing or squeezing air through pipes. The size of the pipe, what it is made of and how it is played all affect the sound of the instrument.

Brass instruments include cornets, trumpets, trombones, tubas and French horns. Players blow into the instrument and use their lips to help make different notes and sounds.

An organ is a wind instrument with a keyboard. The player presses foot pedals to squeeze air through the pipes. The bigger the pipe, the lower the note.

South American Indians in Bolivia play wooden pipes by blowing into them and covering the finger holes.

The bagpipe is just that – a bag fitted with pipes! The player blows air into the bag, then squeezes the bag with his arm to push the air across the pipes fitted with reeds.

The saxophone was invented by a Frenchman, Adolphe Sax, and first used in French army bands. Today, it is often part of jazz or dance bands. It is a brass instrument played by blowing across a reed which vibrates, and by pressing the finger-keys.

The accordion has a keyboard and bellows. The player squeezes the bellows to push air out.

Pollen And Seeds

Plants cannot produce seeds until they have been pollinated. Pollen is carried from one flower to another by wind, water or animals, especially insects. The silver birch tree is a wind-pollinated plant. Its catkins (right) shed their pollen when the wind shakes them.

Plants use wind, water or animals to help scatter their seeds, too. The seeds of the lime tree have a winged case which spins in the air as it falls slowly from the tree. Before it lands the wind may catch it and carry it to a new spot where it can grow.

Dandelion seeds (right) have feathery parachutes and may be carried a long way on the wind.

Mosses produce spores, which are like seeds. The tiny spores are scattered by the wind.

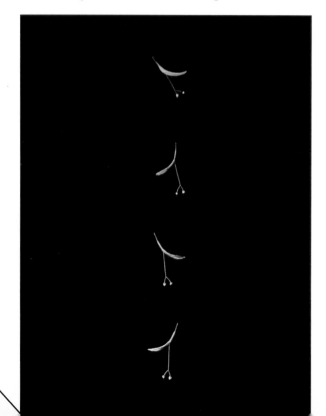

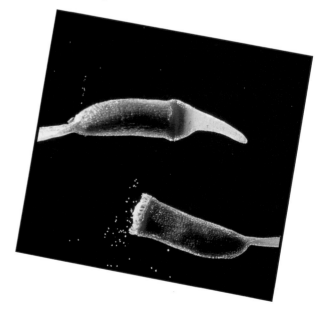

Insect Brooches

Design your own jewellery, based on insect shapes.

Fold a piece of tracing or greaseproof paper in half. Draw or trace one half of an insect along the folded edge, and cut through both thicknesses. Draw round this shape on stiff card and cut it out. Stick or glue a brooch pin on.

Decorate the wings and body with scraps of lace, tissue paper, sequins, feathers, dried leaf skeletons and any other bits and bobs you may have. Use only small amounts of glue for the best results!

Sails In The Wind

Pin-wheels are quick and easy to make. Try using different papers for the sails, and see what happens to the patterns when they spin in a breeze.

1 Cut a square of brightly coloured paper, about 15 cm square (try larger and smaller ones, too).

2 Fold the paper corner to corner to make a triangle.

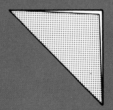

3 Fold the triangle in half.

4 Open out to a square again. Cut in from each corner towards the centre half way along each of the four folds.

5, Now fold alternate corners in to the centre, overlapping the points a little.

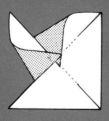

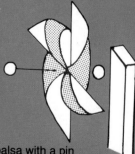

6 Fix the wheel to a thin stick of balsa with a pin (one with a large head is best). A small bead between the wheel and the stick will help the sails to spin freely.

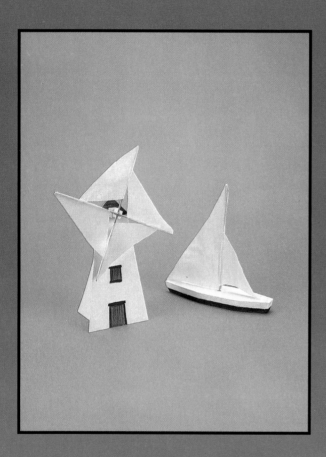

You could make these models of a windmill and a sailing boat, using card, balsa wood, thin dowel and some material for the sails. You could stand them in front of a painted background, showing anything else that can be blown by the wind: trees, washing on the line, smoke from a chimney and so on.

Wind Power

People have used the power of the wind for thousands of years to push boats along. Sailing boats were first used in Ancient Egypt, on the Nile River, in 4000 BC. Sailing boats were used all over the world for trade, exploration and war. About 200 years ago steamships began to replace sailing ships. Today, most sailing boats are used for leisure. A few modern cargo ships have been built with sails, controlled by computers. Wind-powered ships may become more important again as fossil fuels run out.

Windmills work as wind blows the sails round. In the past, windmills were used to grind corn, pump water and drive machinery. Many countries still use traditional windmills.

A new kind of windmill makes electricity. Many wind generators together on a "wind farm" make a lot of noise, but they do not pollute the air as other power stations do.

More Things To Do

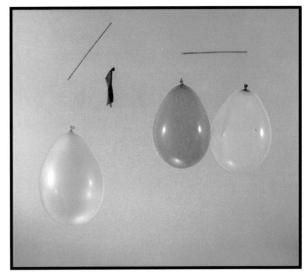

Air is everywhere

Air is all around us. It fills every space it can find, even very tiny spaces. Objects that look solid may have air trapped inside them. You can see this for yourself in a simple experiment. Fill a bucket with clean water. Now gently lower a brick into the water and watch the bubbles of air rise to the surface as the water fills the spaces in the brick. Try the same test with a handful of soil. Can you find anything else that releases air when you put it in the water?

Air is heavy

Try this weighing test to show that air has weight. You need some straws, cotton and some balloons. Tie a blown-up balloon to each end of a straw and suspend the straw so that the balloons balance; then pop one balloon with a pin. Now see if you can make a large balloon balance with a small one.

Air for insulation

Birds keep warm in winter by trapping air in their feathers. Their body heat warms the trapped air. Animals with fur trap a layer of warm air in their fur. People's clothes help to keep a layer of warm air next to the skin. Using air for warmth is called insulation. Can you find places in the house that are insulated?

A Wind Vane

You may have seen wind vanes on churches and other old buildings. A wind vane is marked with points of the compass and tells you the direction from which the wind is blowing. A north wind is a wind blowing from the north, and a south wind is one blowing from the south.

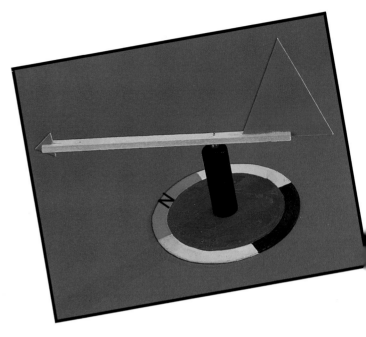

To make your own wind vane, first cut a round base out of cardboard. Mark the base to show north, south, east and west. Glue a round or square piece of wood in the centre of the base. Use a thin stick or a drinking straw for the pointer, making slits at each end to hold the little arrow and tail shape. Fix the pointer to the wood with a strong pin, putting a small bead in between to help the pointer swing freely in the wind.

To try out your wind vane, place it so that north on the vane faces north (to find where north is, remember that the Sun rises in the east and sets in the west). When the wind blows, the small arrow will swing into the wind.

Painting with air

This simple paint spray works as air is blown across the top of the tube dipped in watery paint. Paint is drawn up through the tube as the stream of blown air reduces air pressure in the tube. The spray, which can be bought quite cheaply at a shop selling artists' materials, is fun to use with stencil shapes cut out of paper or card.

An air quiz

1. True or false?
a) Air is a mixture of gases.
b) People take in carbon dioxide from the air.
c) Plants give out oxygen.

2. Name the only mammal that has wings and can fly.

3. Which of these musical instruments is the odd one out?
a) trumpet
b) trombone
c) organ
d) saxophone

4. How are some plants helped by the wind?

5. What is a wind farm?

6. How do birds use air to keep warm in winter?

Air words

How would you describe air, especially as it is invisible? Here are some useful words to start you thinking.

Air on the move	Moving through the air	The feel and smell of air
breeze	glide	heavy
wind	float	light
gale	fly	damp
tornado	fall	smoky
current	hover	clear
draught	soar	sparkling
whirlwind	dive	fresh
shriek	lift	stale
wail	dart	sultry
whisper	plunge	hazy
roar	swirl	crisp
howl	sway	simmering
whistle	spin	
humming	drift	
throbbing		

Index

Air quiz answers

1.　a)　True.
　　b)　False.
　　　　People take in oxygen.
　　c)　True.

2.　The bat is the only mammal that can truly fly.

3.　c)　is the odd one out. All the others are brass instruments.

4.　The pollen and seeds of some plants are spread by the wind.

5.　A wind farm is a collection of modern windmills (wind generators) used for making electricity.

6.　Birds trap warm air in their feathers.

PRINTED IN BELGIUM BY
proost
INTERNATIONAL BOOK PRODUCTION